SOBRIETY & RECOVERY

COLORING BOOK

THIS BOOK BELONGS TO:

....

....

FUCK
ADDICTION!

Look at me
Getting
SOBER
And Sh!t

Sobriety
Isn't An
Anchor!
It's A Pair
Wings!

WELCOME
TO YOUR
NOW!

Rise.
Heal.
Overcome.

KEEP
MOVING
FORWARD

HOORAY!
Another
SOBER
Day

ONE
DAY
AT
TIME

Not Ashamed of my Story. It will Inspire Others.

NOT TODAY
SATAN!
NOT
TODAY

Addicted
to my
Recovery!

Don't Be An
ASSHOLE!
MAKE
AMENDS!

SOBER
AS
FUCK

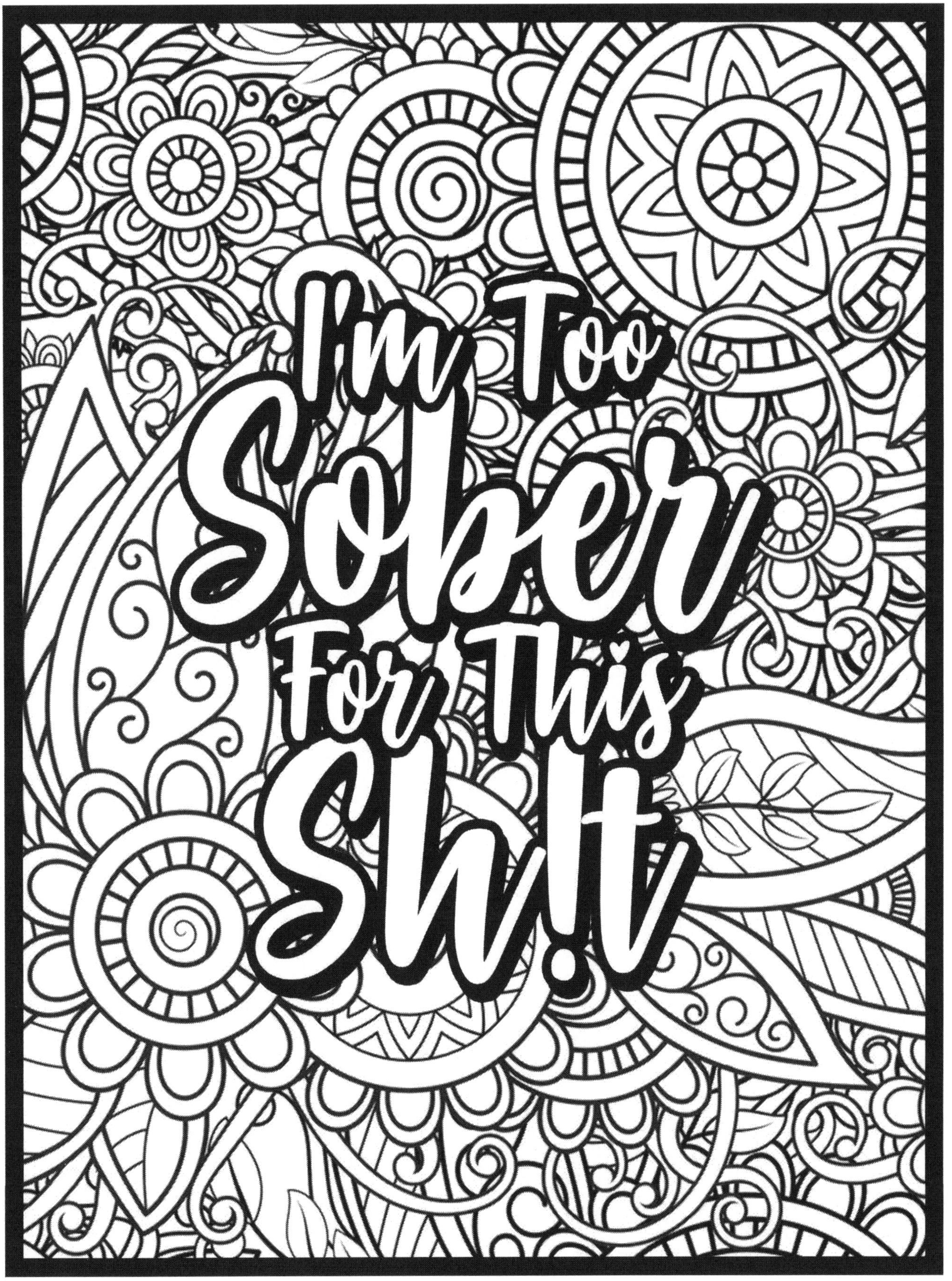
I'm Too
Sober
For This
Sh!t

Strength
in my
Struggle

IT WORKS
IF
YOU WORK
IT

Sobriety
is
Sexy

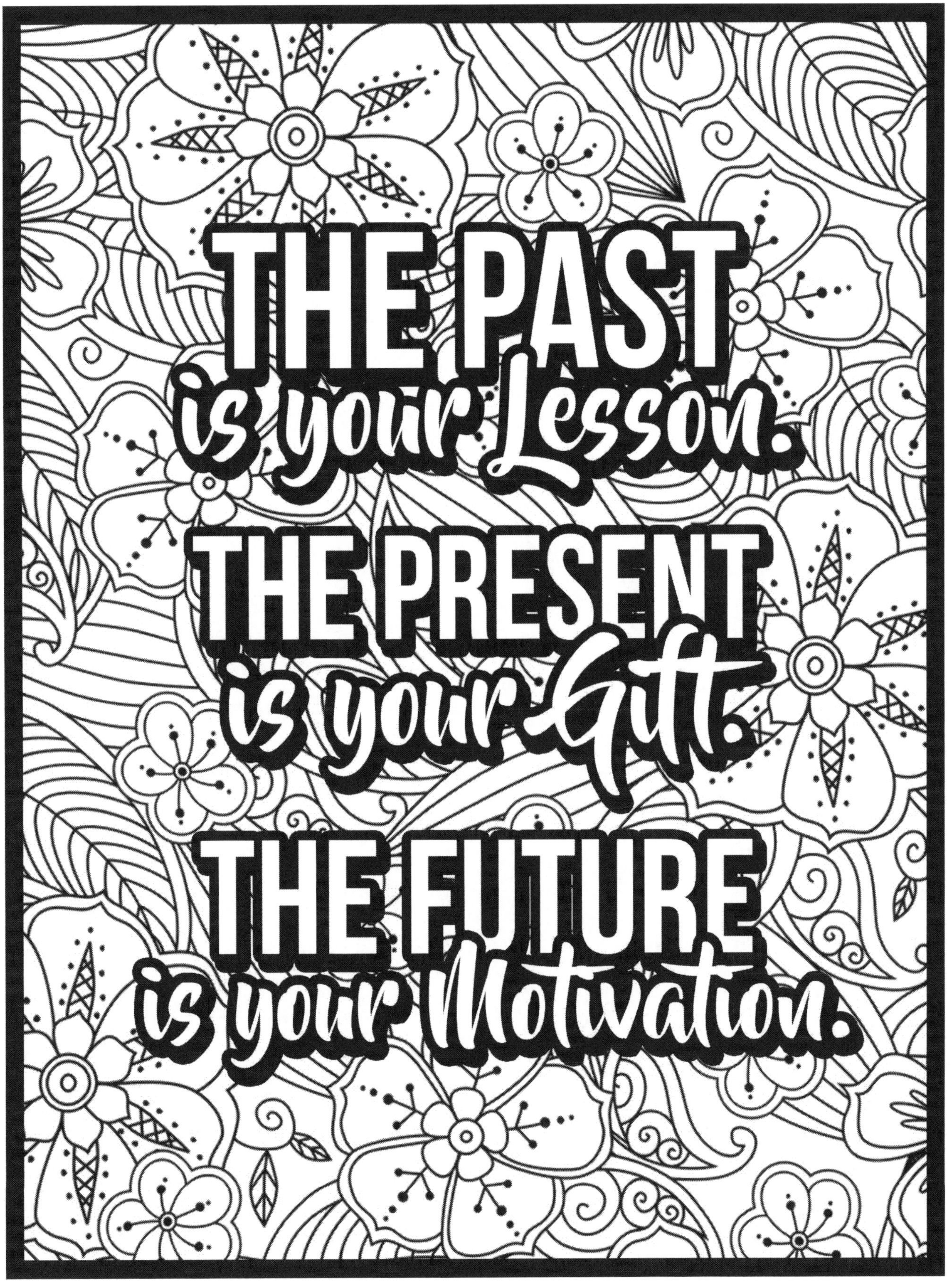
THE PAST
is your Lesson.
THE PRESENT
is your Gift.
THE FUTURE
is your Motivation.

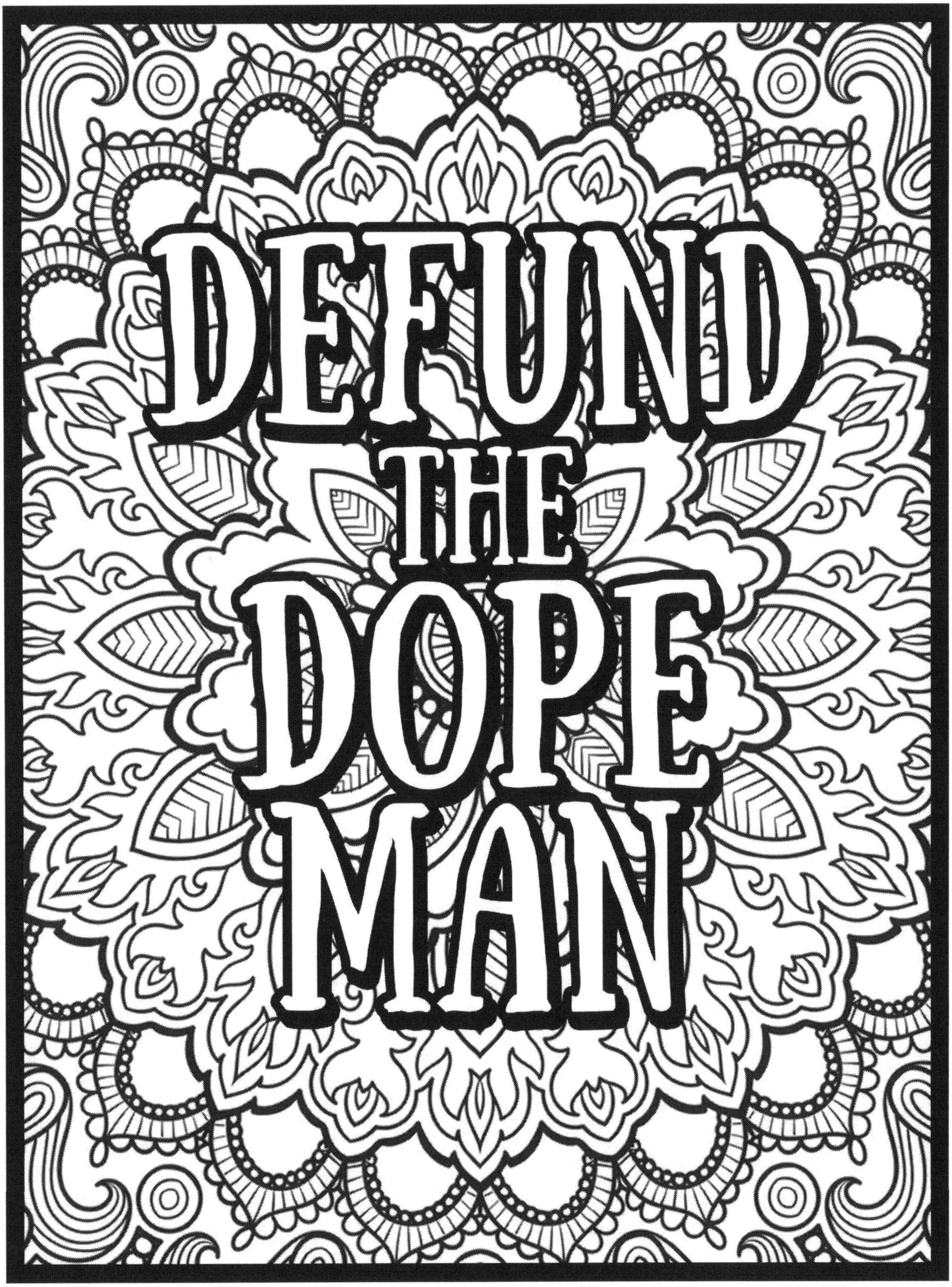
DEFUND
THE
DOPE
MAN

RECOVERY
OR
RELAPSE

Not
Usin'
Boozin'
Losin

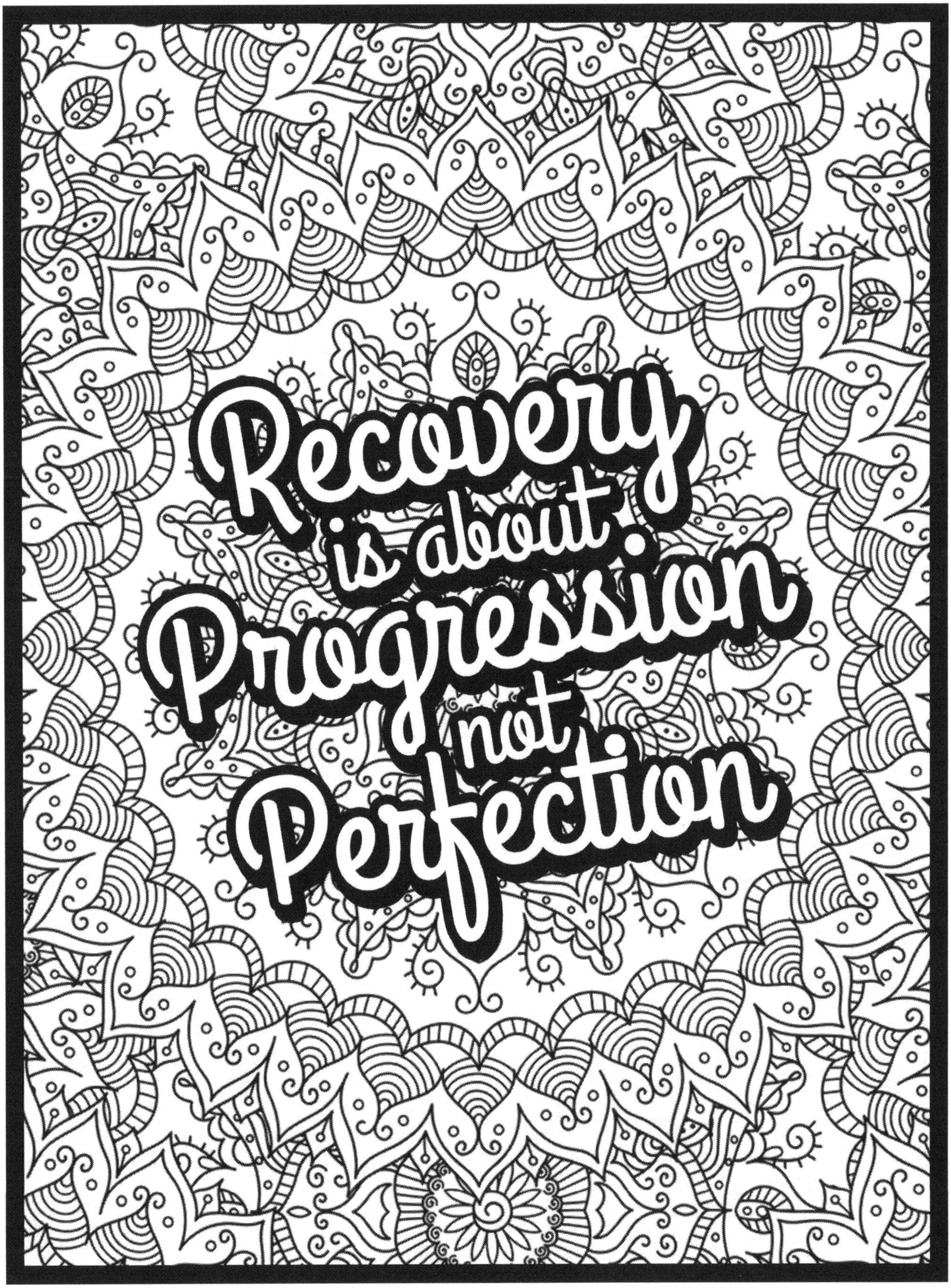
Recovery
is about
Progression
not
Perfection

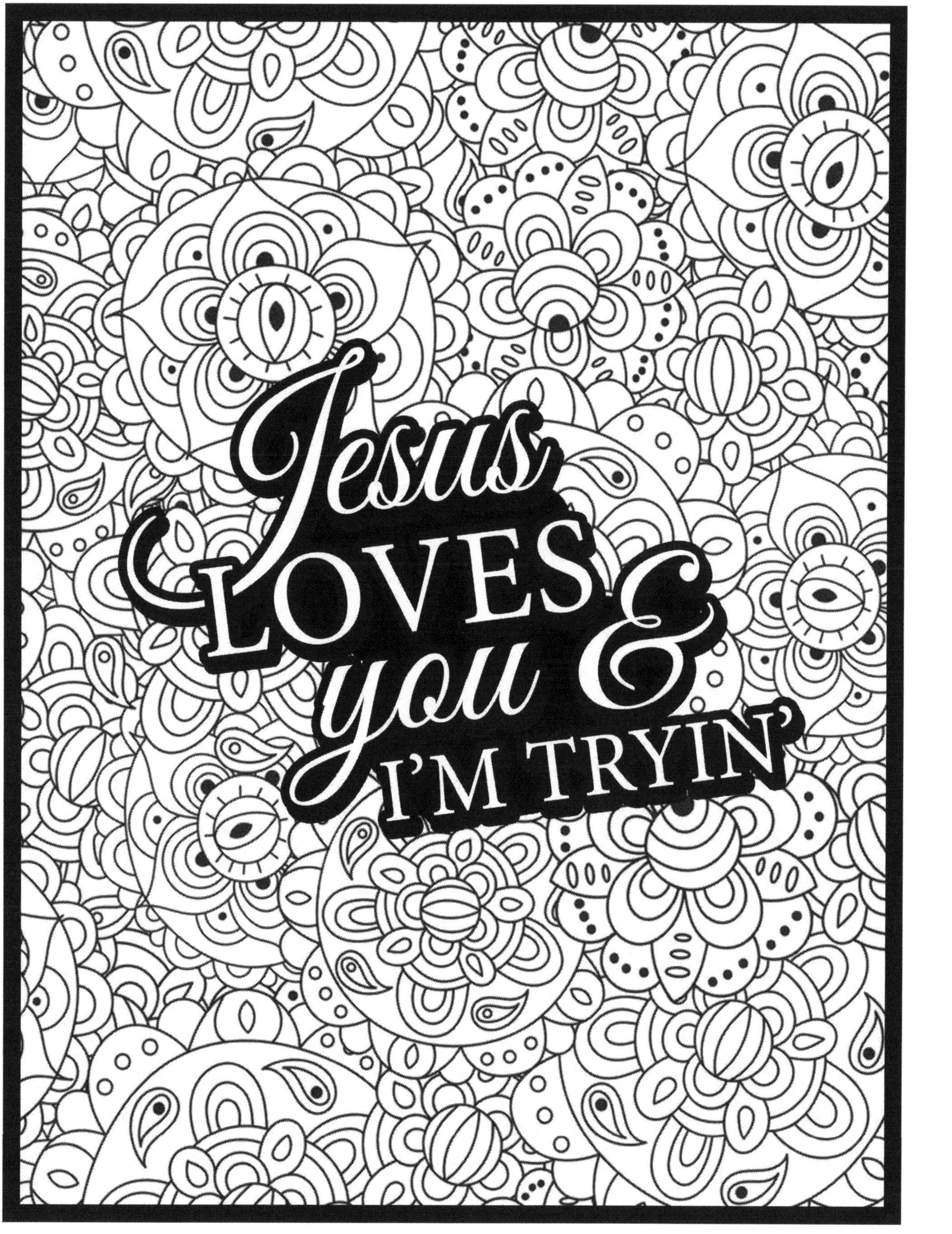
Jesus
LOVES
you &
I'M TRYIN'

Grateful
for
CHANGE!

Made in the USA
Monee, IL
11 July 2022

99505936R00028